Ma
Ser
out of
Sorrow

ALAN G. WEITZMAN *is a rabbi in the Reform movement in Judaism who has specialized in grief processes and is a grief counselor.*

Rabbi Weitzman has conducted seminars and symposia for community-based groups, currently leads several widow/widower support groups, and is involved with volunteer counseling at local hospitals.

He is a founder and a director of a Latino bereavement counseling center and has written articles on case studies in bereavement counseling. Weitzman has been a member of the Association for Death Education and Counseling since 1988.

FOSTER R. MCCURLEY *is a Christian minister of the Evangelical Lutheran Church in America who has specialized in the meaning of the Hebrew Bible and the Greek New Testament for people of faith today.*

For more than twenty years, Foster McCurley was Professor of Old Testament and Hebrew at the Lutheran Theological Seminary in Philadelphia. He also served as a theologian-in-residence on the staff of a national church-wide organization, and he has been a parish pastor. He frequently acts as a consultant to social ministry organizations of the church.

McCurley is the author of fifteen books and numerous articles on themes from the Bible, and on social ministry in today's society.

Making Sense out of Sorrow

A Journey of Faith

Foster R. McCurley
and Alan G. Weitzman

TRINITY PRESS
INTERNATIONAL
Valley Forge, Pennsylvania

Trinity Press International
P.O. Box 851
Valley Forge, PA 19482-0851

Library of Congress Cataloging-in-Publication Data

McCurley, Foster R.
    Making sense out of sorrow : a journey of faith / Foster R.
McCurley and Alan Weitzman.
        p. cm.
    ISBN 1-56338-113-3 (pbk.)
    1. Bereavement—Religious aspects—Christianity. 2. Bereavement—
Religious aspects—Judaism. 3. Consolation. 4. Consolation
(Judaism) 5. Death—Religious aspects—Christianity. 6. Death—
Religious aspects—Judaism. I. Weitzman, Alan. II. Title.
BV4905.2.M23 1995
248.8'6—dc20   95-6281
                                                                              CIP

Printed in the United States of America

95 96 97 98 99   10 9 8 7 6 5 4 3 2 1

To the memory of
Isadore and Ella Weitzman
and
Foster R. McCurley, Sr.

CONTENTS

INTRODUCTION

THIS BOOK IS FOR PEOPLE who are grieving. More specifically, it is for those who in their grieving search for answers to questions that might best be called "religious" — the "God issues," some would say. It is for those who yearn to find hope when their world appears to be falling apart.

The reality of death challenges us beyond the point of our own capability. The realization that each of us will die, the finality of death, our inability to curtail the grief process, our helplessness in comprehending the course of events — all these are part of the agony connected with grief.

In your own grieving you might feel abandoned and alone. You might question: Why, God? Why me, God? Why now? And you look for answers. You reach out for hope and assurance that death is not the last word.

This book addresses the grieving family with the insights of two major traditions, Christianity and Judaism. These traditions assure you that you are not alone in your quest for insights, understandings, and meaning. They, too, wrestle with questions about dying and death, about life and living. Are life and death part of a divine plan of reward and punishment? What kind of justice is it when some suffer and others die without pain? Do you need to accept death without kicking and screaming? Can you look forward to life after death? What is life after death like? How do you move on? This book offers you the opportunity to meet these age-old inquiries with hope and faith. We examine candidly the feelings of guilt, anger, and helplessness. We affirm the value of prayers to God. We encourage you to reach out in faith to God and in trust to family and friends.

Most of all, we challenge all who grieve to walk through the valley of death in order to continue a journey of life that constantly grows under the loving care of God.

Chapter One

WHY?

NOTHING TORMENTS us more deeply than the death of someone we love. Losing a loved one throws life into a tailspin. It also raises a host of questions. Often among these is the most perplexing question of all: Why?

Making Sense Out of Death

Death forces us to struggle for meaning and to make sense out of what has happened. Without such wrestling you might have difficulty regaining your balance, finding some direction, overcoming your despair. Perhaps you think that if you can understand why, you'll adjust better to the new circumstances death has thrust upon you.

Difficult though it is, the struggle to understand can be a healing balm in the midst of a crisis. Without such struggling, you might never deal adequately with what has happened.

The human tendency is to deny that death has occurred and to fail to acknowledge the

---

In reality everything has changed — your plans, your role, your dreams.

---

finality of its sting. In the midst of all the physical and emotional exhaustion that accompanies death, some people refuse to accept it and yearn for life to go on as it always has.

Yet, in reality everything has changed — your plans, your role, your dreams. You can allow your understandable depression over all the changes to deprive you of the strength and desire to move ahead with your life. Or, you can participate in the journey that can lead you to growth and fulfillment.

But where do you turn for answers? Who will respond to the thousands of questions you have been raising in your solitude? Maybe you'll decide to talk to the doctors and nurses. Maybe you'll seek out a counselor or a clergy person. Maybe you'll want to go straight to God.

Daring to Ask God

You might have been taught to accept whatever God throws your way and not question it. Perhaps someone has told you that the death over which you are grieving is God's will and that you should quietly accept whatever has happened. But the death of a loved one raises agonizing questions. God will not punish you for asking questions. Ultimately, you will find that asking has led you toward healing.

Why, for example? Why did such a good and kind person die? Maybe you have already questioned your own sense of worth and wished that you had died instead, that you deserve death more than your beloved. Maybe you've been thinking about other people, ones you believe deserve to die, people you know or people you have read about or seen on television. They go on living, while good people die. Where is the justice?

In the world we expect to live under a system of reward and punishment. Good people should be rewarded for the things they do, and bad people should be punished. We learned the system as children. We know that life should

---

> *Why does God allow it to happen? Or did God make it happen?*

---

work that way, and we get upset when we do not see justice in the world.

How the injustice of it all hits home when someone so good and beloved dies! Why does God allow it to happen? Or did God make it happen? Was God angry at your beloved? Is God punishing you?

Did God take away someone you love in order to test your faith? Or to refine you? To discipline you? We have all heard that adversity strengthens a person. We know, too, that a strict teacher who insists on discipline and hard work in a classroom often gets the pupils to perform exceptionally well. Maybe you have wondered if the purpose of it all is to stir up in you a different set of values. We know that nothing causes us to deal with our own mortality like the death of someone we love. Is that what this death is about? To make you think more seriously about life and death?

Somewhere along the way you've heard that God is all powerful, all knowing, all loving. How does that religious teaching fit with the death you are mourning? Why didn't God intervene with just a little of that power, one little miracle, to keep your loved one alive? Why didn't God share a little of that knowledge to warn you and your beloved what would happen? How could a loving God cause or even allow such pain and grief?

Such questions can make you feel very much alone. They are not the kinds of questions you feel you can share with friends, even with other members of the family. It is bad enough that your loved one left you alone. It is even worse when you think you are left to yourself to deal with your confusion.

Alone With Universal Questions

Nothing makes us feel as lonely as suffering does, whether it be physical or emotional. The loneliness is there even in the midst of family and friends. Even though they say, "I know how you feel," they do not. They cannot. They are not in your shoes. Your pain, your grief, your questions are unique.

In another sense your questions are universal. They are feelings and fears and questions that have been raised by people everywhere and at all times. They have been asked about God. They have been raised to God. They have been preserved because they belong to everyone.

Some of the earliest writings known to humanity are ones that struggled with the reasons people suffer and die. One ancient text from the Middle East, more than 3,000 years old, questions why a man, wealthy and of noble birth,

These proverbs seek to provide simple answers to complex questions, to provide direction for people, to explain the mysteries of life.

has suddenly experienced a series of tragedies that have robbed him of his dignity. At the end the man recognized that the ways of God are unfathomable.

Sometimes people look for answers to those perplexing problems about suffering in easy-to-remember proverbs handed down from generation to generation. "The evil you do returns upon your own head," one of them teaches. "You only get what you deserve," says another.

Still another tells us, "You only get what you can bear."

The Bible contains an entire book of proverbs. These proverbs seek to give simple answers to complex questions, to provide direction for people, to explain the mysteries of life. They are based on the simple notion that the wicked are punished and the good are rewarded. Certainly this is one way to explain why some people suffer: they must be counted among the wicked and are receiving their just desserts.

The biblical Book of Job, too, contains much of that understanding. Proverbial wisdom was what the friends of Job offered him in his misery. He is suffering; therefore he must have done something wrong.

Job does not accept that answer. The answer does not fit human experience. Good people suffer. Wicked people flourish. When God finally comes to Job after so much unhelpful advice from his friends, God overwhelms him. God speaks to Job about wisdom and power and awe. But nowhere does God take the credit or the blame for causing human suffering!

In a single day Job lost his flocks and his servants, then even his sons and daughters. He confessed at the beginning of the story, "the Lord gave, and the Lord has taken away; blessed be the name of the Lord." Though the violence was caused by murdering enemies and natural disasters, initially Job attributed the deaths to God. At the end he was not as certain about his answers, but he praised God even more.

In his encounter with God, Job discovered three things about his own suffering. First, that God does *not* will suffering and death. Second, that suffering is not the direct result of a person's sins. Third, that many questions still remain unanswered.

First and foremost, the question *why* remained unanswered, but Job learned that God listens to prayers and petitions and even complaints. Job realized anew that God is indeed all powerful, but that God does not use that power to suit our desires. God does not allow us to set the divine agenda but invites us to look at the larger picture of what God intends for life in this world and another.

In the Greek New Testament we hear about Jesus' disciples struggling with the *why* question. They came upon a man born blind, and they asked, "Rabbi, who sinned, this man or his parents, that he was born blind?" Jesus answered, "It was not that this man sinned, or his parents, but that the work of God might be made manifest in him." Then Jesus demonstrated the work of God by enabling the man to see. The will of God, the disciples learned, is for sight and life.

The Big Picture

Why am I suffering like this? Why did my loved one die? Is it God's punishment? God's will? Is God testing my faith? Disciplining me for maturity?

These questions are found in the Bible in one passage or another. The answers provided are

---

God's will is for life, not for death.

---

many, but they are sometimes no more satisfying for us than the ones given in the proverbs. However, the Bible as a whole, literally, from the beginning of the Hebrew Bible to the end of the Greek New Testament, assures us that God's will is for life, not for death. We see, too, that God is a gracious and forgiving Parent, not a stern and vengeful Judge.

When God created the world and everything in it, God made human beings with worth and dignity. To live out that dignity God gave humans a place to live, food to eat, other persons for community, and fruitful labor. There was no pain. There was the opportunity for life, a tree of life, in the Garden of Eden that God made. That is the way the Bible begins, and it shows us God's will for life and wholeness.

The Hebrew Bible contains the preaching of the prophets, those people God sent to speak the truth about God and God's ways.

If God's will is for life, why then does death occur?

Often these prophets talked about a new day to come, a new heaven and a new earth. Isaiah, Amos, Jeremiah, and the others preached sermons about life in that new day. Their portrayals of the new life look exactly like the stories at the beginning of the Bible. God's will, seen from the first and the last, is for life.

Christians believe that Jesus was God's Son and that he came to do God's will. Accordingly, he healed the sick, fed the hungry, gathered a community of disciples, raised people from the dead, and forgave sins. He knew the big picture, and he was already acting as though the end-times were beginning. He also promised the new day would come when all people would experience the will of God. Then God will have the last word.

The Greek New Testament ends with a vision of a new heaven and a new earth. The last chapters of the Book of Revelation promise a time when there will be no pain, no death, no grief. Life is the will of God. Life will be God's last word just as it was the first. As a whole, the Bible shows us a God who desires not death and suffering but life and health.

Then *Why?*

If God's will is for life, why then does death occur? Why are you left to suffer the consequences of grief if God's will is for life?

In Judaism, death is explained as part of God's plan for the universe. Just as the leaves of the tree drop in the fall, so does human life end in due course. Death occurs because humans are mortal, and so dying is part of living. At the same time, however, the biblical understanding of God, that big picture, makes it inconceivable that death is the end of existence and that death marks the end of the relationship we have with God. If death is part of the plan, it is only part. The conclusion of the plan is life, life forever, life with God.

In Christian teaching, death is the result of sin. "The wages of sin is death," the apostle Paul writes. But the death of an individual is not the result of the individual's sins. Rather, everyone is mortal because all humans stand against God as sinners. The result of this universal sin

---

God will have the last word,
the word of life.

---

is universal death. In Christian understanding, the death of Jesus on the cross saves us from the power of our sin, and the resurrection of Jesus from the dead shows God's power over death to give new life. God will have the last word, the word of life, as God already uttered it when Jesus was raised from the dead.

Why your loved one died can only be understood within this big picture. We do not know why he or she died in this way and at this time. But even without the answers, God gives us the hope of new life, courage to continue with the present one, and the promise of the divine presence as we struggle onward here and now.

God With Us

The promise that God will be present with us through all kinds of situations fills the Bible. That presence of God enables us to face the difficulties life and death bring. "God with us" gives courage and strength and hope even when everything seems to stand in our way.

The Bible tells us that Jacob, the son of Isaac, had to leave home because he had cheated his brother Esau repeatedly. At his mother's suggestion Jacob headed for the home of his uncle Laban. On the way Jacob had a dream about

> *"I will be with you"* on *the journey, no matter how difficult it might be.*

the angels of God going back and forth from heaven to earth. In the midst of the dream God announced to him, "I will be with you wherever you go, and will bring you back to this place." The good news here is that even to one who was guilty of cheating his brother, God promised to be present in the strange unknown place to which he was going.

When God told Moses he was to go back to Egypt to bring the people of Israel out of their slavery, Moses objected on the basis of his own unworthiness. "Who am I that I should go?" he asked. God answered his question only with the promise, "I will be with you" on the journey, no matter how difficult it might be.

When God announced to Jeremiah that he was to be the Lord's prophet, the man objected because of his youthfulness and inexperience. God dealt with that feeling of inadequacy by promising him as well, "I will be with you."

At his birth Jesus was called Immanuel, "God with us," because Christians believe God was present in this man, even from his infancy. Jesus is called the Word-made-flesh because it is one way to talk about the presence of the eternal God in him, a human being sharing our human nature, experiencing many of our human limitations, even death itself. When he was raised from the dead, Jesus met with his apostles to commission them to spread the news about him throughout the world. The task was difficult, dangerous, and worldly unrewarding, but Jesus promised, "I will be with you to the close of the age."

What can we do without having the answers we want so desperately? In spite of the Bible's own struggling with the *why* questions of pain and suffering, we look to a God whose will is for life. That God is one who promises to be with us at all times, never to leave us alone, even in our suffering. That God is one who promises us new life.

That God is also the one who can bring good even out of the worst of situations. Even though God did not cause the death of your beloved, God can work in you new understandings, lead you in new directions, enable you to grow through the pain and the sorrow into a person who has even more to give to life than you might ever have thought before.

The Value of the Struggle

Many questions about life and death cannot be answered, but they should be asked nevertheless. In this lifetime we will never fathom some of the mysteries of human existence. But the quest, in spite of the struggling it brings, is itself part of the process of healing and wholeness.

Trials and tribulations, no matter what causes them, can provide the opportunities for God to reach out to us and for us to reach out to God. They can challenge our faith and lead us on the necessary journey to acceptance, hope, and healing.

The road to healing is as personal as the quest itself. What works for one person might not work for another. The timetable differs from one person to another, too. Some parts of the journey might take longer for you than for others. At times the progress might be swift, and at other times the direction might be reversed. The precise path might not be clear. A great deal of patience is necessary until you reach that point where you can reinvest in your own life and start anew.

One thing is certain: you are not alone on your journey. "I will be with you" are the words of God, even to people who feel unworthy or incapable of the task. That promise comes from a God who is loving and forgiving. The God who is present with us is one who invites our prayers, even our anger, and gives us hope.

Chapter Two

PRAYER

WALKING THROUGH THE VALLEY, bereft of your loved one, has confused you, angered you, saddened you, and challenged you. On the one hand, you feel the need to be strong, particularly in front of other family members and friends. On the other hand, you want to tell the story of your loss and your hurt again and again, to pour it all out. How can you be strong for others when deep inside you know you are more vulnerable than ever before in your life? Where do you turn?

Perhaps you are becoming concerned that people will tire of hearing about the death and your sadness. You might burden yourself with the perception that your message is depressing them and they need to get on with their lives. You do not want to experience their rejection; the death of your loved one might already feel like rejection. Alone and isolated, you might not know where to turn.

There is small comfort in realizing this is a journey everyone takes. You need more than company in your sorrow. Where can you get what you need?

Suppose you are having trouble finding the right words to describe your feelings. You are

---

> *Alone and isolated, you might*
> *not know where to turn.*

---

angry, dejected, forsaken. You feel vulnerable. You are plagued by irrational thoughts. Where can you turn for help?

Invitation to Prayer

People throughout the ages have found comfort and solace in turning to God in prayer. One of the advantages of prayer is that it does not require eloquence or fixed form or even a logical sequence of words. Another advantage is the variety of settings in which you can offer your prayers — public or private, at home or in the car or in a forest or a field. Communication with God can take place anywhere and at any time. Prayer gives a freedom of expression we cannot find anywhere else.

God wants our prayers. Prayer is one of the ways we can be completely honest with God, and through that honesty comes the relationship God always seeks with us. Prayer allows us to dump our deepest and most secret thoughts and feelings on the one who desires us to come for comfort and healing.

The Psalms of the Bible abound with invitations to take your troubles to God.

Cast your burden on the Lord,
  and he will sustain you (Psalm 51:22).

The Lord is a stronghold for the
    oppressed,
  a stronghold in times of trouble.
And those who know your name put
    their trust in you,
for you, Lord, have not forsaken those
    who seek you (Psalm 9:9–10).

As a result of these invitations and expressions of confidence, people turn in their desperation to offer their deepest thoughts and feelings in prayer. Listen to the honesty and the desperation voiced by a person in dire need of God's comfort.

Be gracious to me, O Lord, for I am in distress;
    my eye is wasted from grief,
    my soul and my body also.
For my life is spent with sorrow,
    and my years with sighing;
my strength fails because of my misery,
    and my bones waste away (Psalm 31:9–10).

These are outpourings of the heart by those who seek God's graciousness. The prayer expressed through this and other psalms has enabled people to bring their innermost feelings to God.

Christians look to Jesus as the model of the prayer life. The Gospel stories tell frequently that Jesus, true to his Judaism, prayed to God often, especially in the midst of difficult times. His prayer in the Garden of Gethsemane prior to his arrest by the Roman soldiers is a model of faith in time of duress. "My Father, if it is possible let this cup (death on a cross) pass from me; nevertheless, not as I will, but as you will." Further, his prayer from the cross for those who crucified him inspire Christians to love their enemies: "Father, forgive them, for they know not what they do."

Jesus encouraged others, too, in the value of

prayer and its power. He taught his disciples a prayer to use in a variety of circumstances. Christians call it "the Lord's Prayer" because it came from Jesus, although there is little that is uniquely Christian about it. It could have been

---

The words let God be God and allow the believer to remain open to God's agenda for life here and now and in the age to come.

---

prayed by others in his own religious tradition, Judaism. The prayer Jesus taught begins with an expression of praise and trust in God: "Our Father who art in heaven, Hallowed be your name. Your kingdom come." Then the prayer expresses the faithful submission of the believer to the will of God: "Your will be done on earth as it is in heaven." The words let God be God and allow the believer to remain open to God's agenda for life here and now and in the age to come.

On another occasion, in order to teach his disciples "that they ought always to pray and not lose heart," Jesus told a parable about a widow who pleaded incessantly with a judge for vindication from her adversary. That persistence, Jesus said, is the model for praying to God: keep at it night and day until God responds. Pray as often as you want or need! That's God's invitation!

The Challenge of Prayer

It is possible that God is the last person you want to talk to at the moment. Perhaps you feel that God is responsible in some way for the death of your loved one. Or, that God could have prevented it. Or, that God did not listen to your prayers when you pleaded for recovery and healing. Perhaps you are even afraid of God, considering what has just happened.

What would it mean, under those circumstances, to pray?

It would mean, above all, that you would expose yourself, your innermost being, to one who is frightening. You would unveil your vulnerability to one who has all the power. The defenses you have worked so diligently to develop would be gone.

All that would be enough to keep you from praying — if you were right about God causing the death to occur, or ignoring your earlier prayers, or overpowering you. But suppose instead that Job was right when he learned that God does not will suffering or death, or punish

> *Suppose that the Hebrew Bible and the Greek New Testament are correct in their understanding that God wills life and that God promises to be present with us even in our trials and tribulations.*

according to individual sins and failures. Suppose that the Hebrew Bible and the Greek New Testament are correct in their understanding that God wills life and that God promises to be present with us even in our trials and tribulations.

What would it mean, then, to pray?

It would mean pouring out your innermost thoughts, even your anger, to a God who loves you. It would mean praying to the God who allows you to enter into the divine presence with the assurance that God is waiting with open arms to set you on a new path, the road to wholeness.

Throughout the Scriptures, whenever people experienced the nearness of God, they backed away in fear, not knowing what would happen next. Each time they were assured that God's presence would not bring them devastation.

"Fear not," the angel of the Lord said to Moses when the Lord appeared in the burning bush to announce God's will of salvation for Israel. "Fear not," the same angel said to Gibeon when the Lord came to send the man on a mission to save the people of Israel from invasions. "Do not be afraid," Jesus said to Peter when he called him to be a disciple after delivering a boatload of fish into his nets. "Do not be afraid," the resurrected Jesus said to the women who came to the tomb on Easter morning.

God's presence, as awesome as it is, is not something to fear, for the God who comes to us is a God of love. In prayer we place ourselves in a position in which God enters into our lives. That God, the one who created all things and all people, comes in prayer not to scare us but to comfort us and move us in new directions.

Are You Ready For This?

The difficulty with prayer, even to such a loving God, lies in the challenges it brings. First of all, in prayer God challenges us to come into that awesome presence with the full realization that God is God and we are not God. We are not in control; God is. We do not understand the agenda; God does. We are not strong; God is.

Prayer gives us the opportunity to recognize who God is and to come before the Lord just as

---

It is comforting to know that God is the one in charge.

---

we are, even overcome by grief. In prayer before God we acknowledge our dependence and our weakness. We can admit our humanness and our feebleness and our failures, and God accepts us lovingly just as we are!

Prayer means letting God be God and letting ourselves be human. That is the first thing that happens in prayer, and it is comforting to know that God is the one in charge.

The second thing that happens in prayer is that God challenges us to move in new directions. If we are willing to admit our frailties and weaknesses before God, then we are opening ourselves to the possibility that God will do something to change us. God is always ready to move into our lives to enable us to become something new, and honest expressions of our weaknesses and limitations give God the opportunity to lead us to somewhere new. The direction is for our good, because our welfare is always the concern of the God who loves, the God of the "big picture," the one who wills life.

Some people, especially in their depression and anger, refuse to admit the necessity of change. Change, they feel, is just one more disruption in their lives, one more adjustment they cannot make. They are afraid of something happening, good or not, healing or not. They

---

Opening yourself to God's new directions will move you from where you are in your grief to growth as a new person.

---

do not want to deal with anything else. They do not care about life anymore. With those feelings they might not pray at all, because when people pray to God, they can expect something to happen.

The psalmist in the Bible puts his expectation in a prayer like this:

Create in me a clean heart, O God,
    and put a new and right spirit
      within me.
Cast me not away from your presence,
    and take not your holy Spirit from me.

Restore to me the joy of your salvation,
and uphold me with a willing spirit
(Psalm 51).

Refusing to change will keep you from making this journey toward restoration and wholeness. Opening yourself to God's new directions will move you from where you are in your grief to growth as a new person. Allowing God to enter your life will lead you forward to healing and wholeness. Such a change occurs because you can take to God in prayer not only your thoughts and anger and disappointment. You can take yourself, the self God loves and wants to heal.

The changes and the challenges God brings might surprise you. When the angel of the Lord urged Moses and Gibeon not to fear the Lord's presence, God sent them on a mission in which they would serve as God's agents for other people. When Jesus comforted Peter at the lake and the women at the tomb with the news that he was not to be feared, he sent them on a mission of life for others.

Being open to God in prayer means not only comfort for yourself in your grief. It also challenges you to plunge into the fullness of life where you can become a source of support and

> *The God who loves you*
> *waits for the opportunity*
> *to enter your deepest and*
> *most shameful thoughts*
> *with love and graciousness.*

strength for others. In that movement you are headed toward wholeness.

Prayer is risky, then, because it opens you to the direction God has in mind, and that path might require you to be different. But what God has in store, surprising though it might be in your moments of despair, is the movement from grief and pain toward wholeness and participation in life.

Private and Communal Prayer

Meaningful prayers can be offered by yourself alone in the privacy of your thoughts or in the company of the congregation. Each method has its advantages, and so you should pray in both ways.

The advantage of private prayer is the opportunity to pour out your heart to God whenever and wherever you want. Whether alone on a walk, or driving in your car, or in the solitude of your bedroom, you can share with God any thought that describes your feelings of the moment. Some of those expressions you might never want to share in the company of others, but you need to express them — disorganized or inarticulate as they might be — and God is always ready to listen. Some feelings you might be ashamed about having and would never want to admit them to other people, but the God who loves you waits for the opportunity to enter your deepest and most shameful thoughts with love and graciousness.

Some of the psalms cited above might help you express such feelings to God — if you'd like such help. Perhaps browsing through the Book of Psalms will enable you to find those that best speak your thoughts and feelings. Many of them are surprisingly candid and might fit your needs precisely.

Communal prayer has its advantages, too. Lifting your voice with others in a congregation of faith helps you to realize you are not alone. People in the congregation have been through the agony of grief, too. They have walked in pain through the valley, as you do now. They know the confusion, the loneliness, and the hurt. They experience the lingering doubts and anger. The good news is that they are moving forward! Among other things, they have found the importance of prayer and all that it offers. And so can you!

Sometimes in the process of public prayer you hear something you had not thought of on your own. Pain and depression can impair our vision. Locked away in our own issues, we often fail to see other sides, other joys, other opportunities for growth. The prayers of others might open your heart to new dimensions for growing and healing.

Among those new dimensions is the opportunity for praise and thanksgiving to God. Alone in your grief you might find little for

You are just as special to God as anyone who has ever uttered this prayer.

which to be thankful. In the company of others, singing and praying and praising, lifting hearts and minds in words and in music, you might discover or rediscover the joy that belongs to people of faith. God invites you to the realization that in spite of the death of your loved one, there is his or her life to be celebrated, your mutual love for which to be grateful, and the spirit of community to support you now.

Above all, public worship makes vivid that you belong in the family of God. You are not alone. You are part of a group, a community of faith, praying together to find firm footing through the valley.

> Even though I walk through the valley of
>   utter darkness,
>   I fear no evil;
> for you are with me;
> your rod and your staff comfort me
>   (Psalm 23:4).

Such is the confident hope of the prayer that has brought comfort to people over the centuries. You can find comfort here, too, for you are just as special to God as anyone who has ever uttered this prayer. You are part of the humanity that the Lord created in the image of God. You possess the same God-given dignity as Abraham, Sarah, Moses, Ruth, Matthew, Elizabeth, and Paul. You are also as weak as any of them, as needy as they were, as fit or unfit for God's grace. You are as privileged as anyone else to come before God in prayer and to say with confidence, "You are with me."

The following prayers might serve as a model for you to formulate your own. The first two are designed for people of the Jewish faith, the latter two for Christians.

Almighty God,

As I mourn the passing of my loved one, may I praise you for the beauty of life; for all that was good and noble that endures in our thoughts and lives on in our deeds. I thank you for those who brought me comfort and counsel; their presence made a difference. For family and friends whose silence and action gave me support and solace, bring healing to their aching hearts and the knowledge that sharing pain brings us together in friendship and love.

Almighty God,

I feel alone and my spirit is broken. In my despair, my days are endless and without meaning. Help me in my weakness to reach out for your support. Let me sense your nearness and experience your love.

Grant me the wisdom to accept myself and others. Cleanse me of all guilt and free me of anger. Give me the vision to see the light and the strength to reach out to you.

Gracious Lord,

I am despaired at all that has happened. Hear my despair and help me. Forgive me for whatever I might have done or failed to do, so that I might be free of the heaviness in my heart. Guide me in the days ahead to act with patience and understanding toward others. Accept my thanks, O Lord, for the love I have known in my life with my beloved. Enable me to celebrate that love by a life of faithfulness now. Strengthen me in the hope of everlasting life when we shall be joined once again. In Jesus' name. Amen.

Merciful God,

Grant that the spirit of Jesus might dwell in my heart, for he knows the pain and the heartbreak I feel. Give me the faith that he showed in his despair and enable me to forgive others as he did. Give me patience and thankfulness, even in my loss, and move me with your compassion and tenderness so that I might treat others with love; through Jesus Christ our Lord. Amen.

Chapter Three

ANGER AND THANKSGIVING

ANGER usually accompanies the death of a loved one. Sometimes we are not aware of the anger pent up within us or its intensity. Sometimes we ventilate hostility at a number of people connected with the dying of those we love. We might even harbor some anger at God.

Angry at Everyone

You might be angry at the doctors and nurses for not being more attentive, more communicative, more caring. You might question their skills, doubt their dedication, and blame them for not saving the life.

You might become annoyed at family and friends for a variety of reasons. You might feel they were not present often enough with the dying person, maybe even question the depth of the relationship they had. You might be disappointed that the children did not express their grief the way you would have expected, or — quite the contrary — that they broke down when they should have been stoic.

You also might become angry when others seem to patronize you. They might say they "understand," that they can identify with your loss, when in reality no one can unless they are in your shoes. Your friends might suggest the death saved your beloved from additional pain and suffering and from a life that would have had no quality. They might try to comfort you with the thought that the suffering and dying were destroying you and your family, when in reality you might feel you should have done more. They might even suggest in subtle ways that "you shouldn't take it so hard," that "everyone dies after all," that "you'll have to get on with your life." They might look uncomfortable when you shed your heartfelt tears as though they were appropriate for the day of the funeral but not for weeks afterward.

You know such friends are trying to be helpful, but often such words only distress you more and even make you angry. You might feel they are not really supportive. They can move on with their own lives, and you are being left behind and alone to deal with your pain.

You might even find at times that the major object of your anger is yourself. Maybe you feel you should have been more alert to the severity of the illness in the early stages and insisted that

---

Maybe you are angry at the changes you need to bear, even changes in your own identity.

---

your loved one go to the doctor immediately. Maybe you regret you did not take more time to spend together when you had the chance. Maybe you feel you did not express your love sufficiently. Maybe you are angry at yourself because you went out of the room and were not present when death struck.

As difficult as it is to admit it, perhaps the anger gets directed at your loved one who has died. She should have fought harder to recover! He was too stoic, or not stoic enough! She should have taken better care of herself!

He should have communicated more clearly his love and appreciation for all you did! She left you alone! He didn't plan sufficiently for the family's financial future!

Maybe you are angry at the changes you need to bear, even changes in your own identity. Suddenly you are a widow or a widower. You might be afraid of how others will perceive you. Will you fit in with others? With your previous life style? What will you do about social activities? Everything had been planned out, your dreams together were coming true, and now you are forced to set new directions for your life. It is enough to make anyone angry.

Angry at God

Where does God fit in your anger? If you believe there is a God who is responsible for life and death, then God might have had a major part in taking away your loved one, and that could make you angry. If you believe in a God who is all powerful, you might be angry that God did not use that power to work the miracle you had hoped for, did not answer your prayers, virtually abandoned you in your time of need. If you believe in a God who has predetermined all things, that your loved one's "time was up," you might be angry that God set the time so soon.

Perhaps swirling in your mind are unspoken issues about the fairness and justice of God. You might be struggling to understand how a good

---

> *If you are angry at God, your greatest difficulty might be admitting it.*

---

and compassionate and loving God could cause your loved one to die and leave you in such a precarious situation. You look around and see all the scoundrels who are still alive and wonder why God has taken away such a good person.

If you are angry at God, your greatest difficulty might be admitting it. You might freely talk to a trusted friend about your anger at doctors and nurses, patronizing friends, distant family members, yourself, your loved one, and the necessity to change your life. But to articulate anger at God sounds disrespectful. It might even make God angry at you.

Unwilling to express anger at God, perhaps you redirect that anger at the clergy person, God's representative, as not being sufficiently supportive or as meddling in your privacy.

Maybe you become angry at your whole religious tradition and reject it precisely at the time when you need the support and comfort and hope that it offers. Maybe you want nothing to do with the congregation you used to attend.

The anger of grief knows no limits. The trauma of losing a loved one can result in subtle or not-so-subtle anger at a variety of people and circumstances. The anger is understandable, perhaps even legitimate. But it needs to be put in perspective.

Anger Re-examined

Family and friends are not usually skilled grief counselors and may indeed in their attempts to be loving and supportive say all kinds of things. They intend their words — outrageous though they seem to you — for support and your well being. Some friends are afraid they might make matters worse, and so they say little or nothing at all. Their silence might have more value than their speaking, for they show they care enough to be present with you even if they do not know what to say or how to say it. Most of us have difficulty dealing with our own grief, to say nothing of helping others with theirs.

All that anger at the loved one you just lost might be misdirected, too. Maybe he found his own way to accept the news of his impending death. Perhaps he thought he was doing you a favor by not discussing it. Maybe she attempted to prepare for her own death, make plans, come to grips with the inevitable, even if you had not seen what she was doing. Perhaps he did not talk about the future because he had confidence in your ability to make it on your own.

As for your anger at yourself for not doing this or that, perhaps your major mistake was

---

The anger we can feel toward God might be based on views we have been taught as children and which keep surfacing through the words of others.

---

failing to hear what the doctor said about the inevitability of death. There was nothing you could have done to prevent it. On the contrary, you might have taken some actions that could have led to false hopes and thus to even more pain. There is nothing to be gained by beating yourself up for failing to do what was beyond your control.

The anger we can feel toward God might be based on views we have been taught as children and which keep surfacing through the words of others. Yes, God does have power over life and death, but that power does not mean that disease and accident and violence and neglect of health and a variety of other causes do not play a part. Yes, God's knowledge is all encompassing, but that knowledge does not mean that God has programmed death for every individual at a certain time as though God were a gigantic computer.

As for the problem we have with God's justice — our loved one dead and less deserving people still alive — we human beings tend to envision God according to our own systems of justice and fairness. Frankly, we do not know the mind of God, neither do we understand God's ways. We can only think in our own limited terms, and we tend to define God by our own human logic. But God is not made in our image. Neither is God confined to our understandings. The Bible acknowledges that truth when it says, "For my thoughts are not your thoughts, neither are your ways my ways, says the Lord."

God's Invitation to Anger

The Bible also recognizes that human inability to understand leads to questioning, doubt, and anger. More important, the Bible offers some ways to express our disappointments and anger at God. In the Book of Psalms there are many hymns and poems that vent such feelings. In fact, these psalms of sorrow and complaint, or psalms of lament as they are often called, are more frequent than any other type of psalm. They are intended to be used by people who look desperately for the Lord's help and, not finding it, complain about God's apparent absence, neglect, and injustice.

Some of these psalms even state their purpose explicitly, like the introduction to Psalm 102: "A prayer for one afflicted, when he is faint and pours out his complaint before the Lord." Some direct that complaint against the seeming absence of God: "How long, O Lord? Will you forget me forever? How long will you hide your face from me? How long must I bear pain in my soul, and have sorrow in my heart all the day?" (Psalm 13).

The prophet Jeremiah uses a psalm like that to complain about his troubles, even blaming God for deceiving him and for making him a mockery in the eyes of his neighbors. He even cursed the day on which he was born. He asked if God were like a "deceitful brook," failing when needed. Jeremiah pleaded that God not continue to be a terror to him.

Jesus, too, used a psalm of lament from the cross. In his physical agony and in face of the

---

Psalms like these were included in the prayer book of ancient Israel so the people had the means and the freedom to complain to God when their suffering seemed unjust.

---

betrayal by his own disciples, Jesus cried the opening words of Psalm 22.

"My God, my God, why have you forsaken me?"

The next lines of the psalm continue the feeling that God has abandoned him in his suffering.

"Why are you so far from helping me,
   from the words of my groaning?
O my God, I cry by day, but you do not
   answer;
   and by night, but find no rest."

Psalms like these were included in the prayer book of ancient Israel so the people had the means and the freedom to complain to God when their suffering seemed unjust, when they couldn't understand what was happening and why, when they couldn't find God present in their lives. They complained not only to God but about God. And the Bible sanctions it!

The good news is that God never punished anyone for getting angry and using these psalms. In fact, Jeremiah, Jesus, and countless others discovered ultimately that God had not abandoned them but was present with them in their sufferings. They came to know that God did work differently, that God's ways were not their ways, and that God's deliverance was not the same kind of rescue from distress they might have desired.

From Complaint to Thanksgiving

Most of the psalms in which afflicted people pour out their complaints before the Lord end with rejoicing and thanksgiving. Having the two pieces — lament and thanksgiving — in the same psalm shows that we can do our complaining with the confidence that God will ultimately deliver, even if that salvation comes in a life after death. The psalm that asked how long God would forget the afflicted one ends on the joyful note: "I will sing to the Lord, because he has dealt bountifully with me" (Psalm 13).

Even while Jeremiah was cursing the day of his birth, he called out,

"Sing to the Lord, praise the Lord!
For he has delivered the life of the needy
    from the hand of evildoers."

The psalm that Jesus began from the cross ends with a celebration of new life, a celebration that takes place at a meal with friends and goes on to include people from all over the earth and from times past and still to come.

The psalms that give freedom to complain even against God are filled with the confidence that God will ultimately work things out according to God's own plans, even if they are not understood by us or experienced in our lifetimes. The psalms of lament assure us that while God's workings are not always apparent to us, especially when we are torn by grief and anger, God is present and powerful, giving us the strength to go on with our lives and the patience to endure grief with hope.

What a wonderful gift God gives! God knows how angry we can become at everything and everyone when death takes away someone we love. God understands that our anger might be directed at family and friends, against the loved one who died, against ourselves, and against anyone who represents God. Knowing all that, the psalms invite us to throw our anger at God, knowing that God has big shoulders and can bear anything we have to say.

In the process of our complaining at God we are admitting how important God is in our lives. When we lament that God has abandoned us, we let God know we need the presence and the compassion that only God can provide. When we cry with the psalms "How long will you hide your face from me?," we acknowledge that even a second without God is too long.

> *In the process of our complaining at God we are admitting how important God is in our lives.*

When we express anger at God for not living up to our expectations, we are confessing that God's will is different from our desires.

God invites our lamenting because God wants our acknowledgement. God permits our complaining because God desires our trust. God allows us our anger because God wants our confessing to bring new perspectives.

Is our anger at God justified? No. It is no more justified than our anger at friends and family, at our deceased loved one, or at ourselves. God does not punish people with death for doing this or for not doing that. God does not abandon us when we need God's strength and presence.

Neither does God punish us for getting angry, even at himself.

On the contrary, God invites us to rejoin that congregation where others, too, have experienced the agony of grief, even felt the forsakenness of God. In the worshiping community God offers us those religious traditions that have helped millions of people to find hope even when life seemed hopeless. In the midst of the congregation's prayers and praises, you can hear again that God does promise to have the last word.

That word is the word of life, and the way to life is ultimately through death. That's the "big picture" again, one that promises eternity.

Perhaps you will find the freedom to express your anger and disappointment in one or more of the following psalms.

Psalm 7	Psalm 25	Psalm 55
Psalm 13	Psalm 26	Psalm 77
Psalm 17	Psalm 27	Psalm 88
Psalm 22	Psalm 31	Psalm 102

Chapter Four

GUILT AND FORGIVENESS

OFTEN WITH GRIEF over losing a loved one comes a sense of guilt. This overpowering emotion might imprison us in a state of depression and dependency. It might block our acceptance of death and our adjustment to a new life. It might impair our judgment in a variety of ways.

Why Do You Feel Guilty?

From where does this guilt come? Some people feel, though often without justification, that they did not do enough, did not demonstrate the depth of their love, did not sufficiently sacrifice, or did not act in a selfless manner. Others might feel that the relationship could have been better, that they should have demanded less, that they should have shared more. They might fault themselves for a thousand small things — "the should have's and could have's" which might have made the relationship more admirable, more harmonious, more meaningful.

Decisions that had to be made in the treatment of a loved one can haunt the survivors afterward. You might be distressed that you did not seek additional and more expert medical opinions. You might regret that you agreed to eliminate "heroic measures." You might think in retrospect that stopping treatment was a premature decision, or that continuing treatment added prolonged pain and suffering. You might be plagued by the decision to remove life supports, the most difficult decision any one has to make about someone they love.

Intellectually you might have accepted the inevitability of the death. You might even acknowledge that your loved one would not have wanted to live on with the impairments to body and mind. Yet signing the papers to let nature take its course can still plague you.

Perhaps there were those moments when you wished death to come because you yourself were being destroyed, torn apart both physically and psychologically by what you were

> *How, after all, does one stand by and witness the dying of a loved one without feeling helpless, out of control?*

experiencing, by the pain and suffering and heartache the dying was inflicting on you. You might not have realized then or now that your experience was normal. How, after all, does one stand by and witness the dying of a loved one without feeling helpless, out of control? It is difficult to realize that seeking relief is part of our desire to preserve our own health and maintain our sanity so that we can continue our own lives and help put together the pieces for family and friends.

Reality Testing

In the process of beginning to extricate yourself from the grip of guilt, you need to test the reality of your expectations about yourself. No one of us has the ability to change the past. Reliving our decisions cannot alter the outcome. The decisions you made were likely the best options for everyone under the circumstances. That is reality.

You need to consider, too, the wishes of your loved one. In all likelihood your beloved would have sanctioned your decisions had he or she been totally aware of the circumstances. You can be certain that the departed knew you acted out of love and compassion and that the decisions were made in the best interest of everyone involved. You did what your loved one wanted you to do, and your acts were courageous. You enabled the one you loved to maintain some dignity and to die in peace. And that is commendable.

Reality also insists that you consider the value of the guilt you are imposing on yourself. It contributes only to compounding the loss. Death has taken one life, and the inability to remove guilt might deny the second as well. If you are stuck on the roadside in the mire of guilt, you will not be able to begin the journey toward acceptance and adjustment. In depression you might desire to remain in darkness, thinking any moments of happiness, joy or creativity are inappropriate for someone who is grieving. You can move toward the light only when you realize your loved one wanted only the best for you, wanted you to reconstruct your life, wanted you to smile again, to work and to play and to be whole.

Forgiveness

In spite of the reality check about the value of guilt, the limitation of our own abilities, and the wishes of loved ones, there are often lingering episodes of guilt. You still might

How do we forgive ourselves?

be convinced you could have done something different. What do you do then?

Ultimately, you need to forgive yourself.

How do we do that? How do we forgive ourselves? Where do we get the authority to wipe away our shortcomings, whether they be actual or only perceived failures?

We start with our understanding of God. The God of Judaism and Christianity is loving and accepting, merciful and compassionate. Stories and teachings, laws and lessons, prayers and hymns from both the Hebrew Bible and the Greek New Testament tell us about the God who forgives.

Long ago, when God brought the people of Israel out Egypt and led them to Mount Sinai, Moses went up on the mountain to receive the stone tablets containing the ten commandments. Down below the people made a golden calf and worshiped it as the god who brought them out of the land of Egypt. When Moses

---

The Lord's forgiveness results in a renewed life, one filled with love and mercy and the Lord's goodness.

---

came down from the mountain and saw what the people had done, he threw down the tablets in his anger and broke them in pieces. Now Moses had to go back up the mountain for another set of commandments. The first thing God said to him on this trip was an announcement about what it means to be God: the Lord is a merciful and gracious God, slow to anger and abounding in committed love. On the basis of that divine nature as "a God ready to forgive" and aware of human frailty, God gave Moses the second set of commandments for the people.

That same understanding of God as one who

forgives is celebrated in the psalms. Listen to them sing out the refrain.

> Yet, he, being compassionate, forgave
>> their iniquity,
>> and did not destroy them.

Again,

> You forgave the iniquity of your people;
> You pardoned all their sins.

So often did the people of Israel experience the forgiveness of God that they defined the Lord as one

> who forgives all your iniquity,
>> who heals all your diseases,
> who redeems your life from the Pit,
>> who crowns you with steadfast love and
>> mercy,
> who satisfies you with good as long as you
> live,
>> so that your youth is renewed like the
>> eagle's.

This hymn praising God shows that the Lord's forgiveness results in a renewed life, one filled with love and mercy and the Lord's goodness. The connection is especially important in showing that the journey from grief to healing begins with the acceptance of God's forgiveness.

To forgive the sins of the community of Israel on a regular basis, the Lord established for the people a system of sacrifices and other rituals. They were the means by which God could wipe away the sins that barred fellowship with God. The day of Atonement, Yom Kippur, is one of the primary festivals for this forgiveness to occur. It is celebrated once a year in synagogues around the world to allow the slate to be wiped clean so that God and the people might

---

The forgiving nature of God also appears as the basic understanding of God in the Greek New Testament.

---

continue their journey together through life, no matter how severe the trials.

The forgiving nature of God also appears as the basic understanding of God in the Greek New Testament. Christians believe that in the death and resurrection of Jesus, God was forgiving the sins of all people, even the ones who executed him on the cross. The early church used different words to talk about the effect of God's forgiveness, words like "reconciliation" (healing rifts among family members) and "justification" (God's declaring people to be innocent even though we are all guilty). The variety of words and images used simply shows that the forgiving nature of God pours out all over the pages of the Greek New Testament so that people of various backgrounds might grasp the good news.

Christians believe that Jesus himself has the power to forgive sins. Indeed, in several stories in the gospels Jesus makes a special point of indicating he had not only the power to heal but also the authority to forgive sins. In Christianity that understanding is possible because of the belief that Jesus is God's Son. Like Father, like Son, when it comes to mercy and forgiveness.

As a way of continuing that forgiveness from generation to generation, Jesus began the sacrament of Holy Communion. This meal, the Lord's Supper, provides the opportunity for those who eat and drink to experience anew the forgiveness God gives through the death of Jesus. In this sacrament, along with other sacraments in the Christian tradition, especially baptism, God's forgiveness flows unceasingly to wipe away guilt and everything else that would get in the way between God and people.

The forgiveness of God we see in the Hebrew Bible and in the Greek New Testament, in present-day synagogues and in the churches,

is the same forgiveness that God offers you.
Whether you feel that you have done something wrong or that you failed to do something
that would have helped your beloved, God
reaches out to you in a variety of ways to wipe
the slate clean so that you can be the whole
person God intends you to be.

Forgiveness Through Prayer

So prominent is forgiveness a part of God's nature, in Judaism and in Christianity, that people
can feel confident about praying for forgiveness for themselves. If a child had a parent who
never granted a request to go outside and play,
the child would cease asking. But if the parent rejoices in the child's interest in exercising
in the fresh air with other children, then the
child's freedom to ask becomes part of the way
of life.

When King Solomon offered his prayer of
dedication at the opening of the Jerusalem Temple three thousand years ago, he recognized that
God could not be confined to that building,
majestic though it was. God continued to live
in heaven as always. And so, five times in the
course of his prayer about the temple, the king
prayed to God in heaven for forgiveness of the
people's sins.

Solomon learned about that freedom to approach God in prayer from the religious tradi-

---

*The ancient hymns often use
language that we feel was
meant for us in our grief.*

---

tion in which he was reared. The psalms used at worship during his time and up to our present time help people vocalize the request for God's pardon and forgiveness. The ancient hymns often use language that we feel was meant for us in our grief.

> Turn to me and be gracious to me;
>   for I am lonely and afflicted.
> Relieve the troubles of my heart,
>   and bring me out of my distresses.
> Consider my affliction and my
>   trouble,
>   and forgive all my sins.

This outpouring of the heart shows faith in a God who loves us, a God with whom we can speak on intimate terms. The direct petition for forgiveness can be made to God, because God is merciful. God invites our petitions so that guilt might be removed. God responds to your confessions, too, for God listens to your concerns and grants you pardon.

I acknowledged my sin to you,
    and I did not hide my iniquity;
I said, "I will confess my transgressions to
        the Lord";
    then you forgave the guilt of my sin.

Having experienced God's forgiveness, the psalmist recognizes the benefits of God's mercy:

Blessed is the one whose transgression is
        forgiven,
    whose sin is covered (Psalm 32:1).

As we saw earlier in our discussion of prayer, Jesus, too, prayed for forgiveness for others, even on those who had crucified him. He said from the cross, "Father, forgive them, for they know not what they do."

Jesus also taught his disciples to pray for the forgiveness of their own sins. In the prayer Christians have come to call "the Lord's Prayer," Jesus taught them to include "And forgive us our debts." It is part of the model prayer for Christians, and in it Jesus invites us to seek God's forgiveness for whatever we have done or not done or feel guilty about.

Forgiving One Another and Ourselves

The petition in the Lord's Prayer "forgive us our debts" continues with the understanding that we forgive those who have sinned against us. The verse following the prayer in Matthew's Gospel has Jesus explain more specifically that as we forgive one another, God will forgive us, and as we refuse to forgive one another, God will not forgive us.

The connection between receiving God's forgiveness and forgiving one another occurs often in the Bible. In the well-known and beautiful story of Joseph and his brothers we see that connection. Because of their jealousy over their perceived favoritism by father Jacob for Joseph, the brothers sold Joseph to a caravan headed for Egypt. Their horrible act led to years of trouble and suffering for Joseph. When at the end of the story his brothers came to him, they asked for his forgiveness. At first, Joseph was appalled at their request, for he, after all, was not God. It was God's right and nature to forgive. However, when he reflected on what God had accomplished through the whole tragic entanglement, he promised to provide for his brothers and their families; "he reassured and comforted them."

An old teaching in the Book of Proverbs tells that

Whoever forgives an offense seeks love,
   but whoever repeats a matter alienates
      a friend.

With such traditions behind him, then, it is no wonder that when the disciple Peter

> *There is no limit to the forgiveness we give to one another because there is no limit to the forgiveness God gives to us.*

asked Jesus how many times he should forgive someone who sins against him, Jesus said "seventy times seven." The answer is not simply a matter of multiplication; it's an expression of infinity.

There is no limit to the forgiveness we give to one another because there is no limit to the forgiveness God gives to us. Christians are called to "forgive one another, as God in Christ forgave you." Within Judaism the pardoning of one another is based on the nature of God who is merciful and loving and forgiving.

In the previous chapter we spoke of the anger you might bear at doctors and nurses, family and friends. Whether they could have done more or not, forgive them. They are human beings with the same limitations you and all others have. Just as you need forgiveness to begin your journey toward healing, so do they, for death and grief affect them, too.

We talked, too, of the anger you might feel at your loved one for leaving you and causing so much turmoil in your life. Forgive him or her, too, for forgiveness is the basis for life under God. Even more, the love and concern your beloved had for you assures you that he or she forgives you, too, for whatever you think you did or did not do. It is the nature of love to forgive.

At the same time, you need to forgive yourself. More to the point, you need to avail yourself of the forgiveness of God. You can experience God's forgiveness by reading your scriptures, by praying in private and with a community of faith, by hearing other people announce what God is inviting you to hear: that God is merciful and forgiving and loving and compassionate to all people, and that includes you. Even in your grief. Especially in your grief.

The more you avail yourself of God's forgiveness for the guilt you feel, the more quickly you will proceed on the path to wholeness. Every time you hear about what God has to offer you, you take one more step toward a new life.

Chapter Five

HOPE AND ETERNITY

THE GOAL OF THE JOURNEY through the pain of grief is life. What enables you and others to move through the unanswered questions, through the anger, and through the guilt to reach that goal is hope.

Hope as Trust

According to popular definition, hope is the expectation that something good will happen. People express their hopes freely and often.

They wish for things that are good and satisfying and fulfilling. Some hope that the sun will shine during the family picnic scheduled for the weekend. Many hope their children will grow up through the teenage years to become contributing members of society. Others hope their

---

Hope is trust in God even when everything seems hopeless.

---

team will win the World Series or the Super Bowl or the Stanley Cup.

In the religious traditions of Judaism and Christianity hope is more than wishful thinking. Hope is confidence that God will be faithful to the promises about being with us in our loneliness, about forgiving us of our failures, and about giving us life forever. Hope is trust in God even when everything seems hopeless. Hope is the assurance that God has the last word, and the word is life, even in the face of death.

What It Means To Be Human

Over the years many attempts have been made to distinguish humans from the rest of the creatures God made. A common saying teaches that "it is human to err," and while the statement is true, it does not help us understand our distinctiveness. Anthropologists have looked for the distinct human quality in the flexibility of the thumb or the use of tools to accomplish various tasks. Philosophers have concentrated on the ability to reason, and others have found the human difference in the ability to look toward the future.

The Hebrew Bible and the Greek New Testament define humanity in relationship to God. First, the Bible teaches that human beings were made to be the image of God in the world, granted dignity, and made responsible to God for all other creatures. Second, the Bible tells us that, though special, we human beings are mortal. Third, we learn that, though mortal and undeserving, we are loved by God now and forever.

The love of God accounts for the reason God made us. The same love assures God's presence with us, even in our worst times. And the love that created us and sustains us does not disappear at death; it creates us anew.

To be truly human is to live with the confident hope that just as God has loved us since birth, God will love us forever.

God's Will for Life: Resurrection

In the first chapter of this book we indicated the need to focus on "the big picture," the view that looks beyond pain and sorrow and grief and death to life with God. We indicated several times throughout the book that the will of God is not for death but for life. That divine will occurs not by removing our mortality but by giving us eternal life through death and in spite of death.

Two exceptions to human mortality appear in the Hebrew Bible. The first was the man named Enoch. In a time long ago, before the time of recorded history, Enoch "walked with God." The man's intimacy with the Creator leads to his being "taken" by God into another world, another time, another existence. The act remains an unexplained mystery, but even the limited number of words announces that God has power over death and wills life. The second exception is Elijah who was taken up alive in a whirlwind to heaven to be with God forever.

Apart from these two individual exceptions to mortality, God extends the hope of eternal life to others by promising life after death. The Book of Daniel ends with the joyous vision that those who are faithful to God in the midst of trials and temptations will be resurrected to be with God.

> Many of those who sleep in the dust of the earth shall awake, some to everlasting life, and some to shame and everlasting contempt. Those who are wise shall shine like the brightness of the sky, and those who lead many to righteousness, like the stars forever and ever.

From prophecies like this and from other truths, Judaism developed the idea that the resurrection of the dead would occur when the

---

Human beings are too important to God, too loved and too precious, to allow death to be the end.

Messiah would appear, and that belief has been reinforced by the rabbis of long ago and by Jewish philosophers over the centuries. The belief in resurrection of the body was combined in traditional Judaism with the notion of the immortality of the soul. When a person dies, the body is buried while the soul goes to heaven to be with God. On the day of resurrection the body is reunited with the soul, and the whole being lives eternally with God. The doctrine affirms the teaching that human beings are too important to God, too loved and too precious, to allow death to be the end.

For Christians the resurrection of Jesus from the dead demonstrates God's victory over death and paves the way for the resurrection of God's people to occur when Christ returns to earth. This belief in resurrection indicates that Jesus Christ is alive and present now, and at the same time it promises new life for those who follow in faith. The confident hope that God will one day take home all who have died is celebrated every Sunday in Christian churches, for every Sunday is a celebration of Easter. This belief makes Easter the most important festival for Christians throughout the world. In fact, without Easter there is no Christianity.

These traditional beliefs in resurrection indicate that for Judaism and for Christianity God wills eternal life. Though death has its sting, God will have the last word. That message is not simply for everyone else; it is for you, too. It's a message that offers you hope — not wishful thinking — precisely when you need the assurance that your loved one will live again.

That new life will be one of beauty and harmony. It will be a life without sickness and pain and sorrow, without grief and dread. It will be a life in the company of many others, and you will be there, too. You and your beloved will be together again in the presence of God.

God's Will for Life: Other Views

Within Judaism and Christianity other views developed besides these traditional ones in resurrection. Some people believe there is a soul in everyone of us that longs to break loose from the mortal body and to return to heaven from where it came. The soul in this view is immortal, the body is basically unimportant, and so immediately upon the death of the body, the immortal soul goes to live eternally with God.

In still other variations the immortal soul moves from one living creature to another, leaving the body of the deceased to find a new habitat, either in another person or in an animal. We call that idea reincarnation. Some religious groups have tried to explain violence and evil in this way, suggesting that people who are wicked now possess souls that in the previous life inhabited the bodies of wild and vicious beasts.

What lies behind all these views is the conviction that human life is too important to end with physical death. Life must go on, and the many attempts to answer how that occurs are ways to offer comfort and hope in the face of death. To think that the life of a loved one continues beyond the grave assures those who mourn that death is not the victor. Life in heaven, life with God, life in a new form — all point to immortality.

Where Is My Beloved Now?

In the traditional views about resurrection at the last day, many people wonder where their

---

So where precisely are we while we await the day of resurrection?

---

beloved is now. If resurrection occurs all at once and for all people at the same time, what is happening to my beloved? What will happen to me?

Judaism and Christianity hold that we are all mortal. We all die, and there is no escape from that reality. Expressions like "He's only asleep" or "She's resting" tend to blunt the harsh reality that we die. There is a finality to death that we all need to acknowledge, even while we wait in confident hope to be raised to life eternal.

So where precisely are we while we await the day of resurrection?

In one sense we do not wait, as though we are waiting expectantly for our daughter's wedding or waiting patiently for the year of retirement or waiting impatiently for relief from a burden. Death removes our conscious waiting. We are no longer disturbed by the passing of time. When we sleep soundly, we awake amazed at how long we slept, how quickly the night passed. Death is like that sound sleep. We die, and the next thing we know, God makes us alive again.

It is appropriate, therefore, to think that as soon as your beloved died, he or she went to be with God. When you die, you will also be with God. Your beloved is in the hands of God immediately, and when you die, you will be in God's hands also. When he or she awakes, you will be there, waking up, too. The passing between death and life is instantaneous as far as the deceased are concerned. Only those who are still alive are entrapped in the world's sense of time, wondering where and how and when. Your beloved is relieved of all that, cradled in the hands of God, loved and cherished by God, as you will be, too.

What Will Life Eternal Be Like?

Our natural desire to know what lies ahead in eternity drives us to ask more than can be answered. No one has come back from the dead to describe what the new life is like. Some people talk about having "near death" experiences, but "near death" is not death. The precise nature of life-after-death remains one of the wonderful surprises God has in store for us.

Within Judaism rabbis and philosophers described the Messianic Age in a variety of ways. According to some, it will be a time when war, famine, jealousy, and strife will disappear in favor of blessings and comforts. Some look to the time as an occasion for miracles, and others portray the age as one in which there is no servitude to foreign powers.

Christians believe there *is* one person who died and was raised to life, and he is Jesus. They look to the records about Jesus' appearances after death for some hint about the nature of the resurrected body. He was recognized by some to whom he appeared, but his appearance must have changed somewhat. He entered rooms with locked doors; yet he was not a phantom, for his disciples could touch his flesh. He ate, and he enjoyed fellowship.

Apart from these reports about Jesus' resurrection appearances, the Greek New Testament offers a few other portrayals of the life to come. The Book of Revelation speaks of a great multitude, people from every nation, surrounding the throne of God and singing God's praises. The same book tells of the heavenly Jerusalem coming down to earth, a city resplendent with the light that comes from God and from the

> *Whatever the precise nature of life hereafter, both Judaism and Christianity agree it will be a better life.*

Lamb, Jesus Christ. According to this vision, paradise will look like the original Garden of Eden but even better: a crystal bright river with a tree of life on each of its banks for the healing of all people.

Christians confess simply and explicitly the assurance that God will raise the dead in the words of the Apostles' Creed: "I believe in the resurrection of the body." This confession offers hope both for the dead and for the living, for it promises reunion with loved ones in the presence of God.

Whatever the precise nature of life hereafter, both Judaism and Christianity agree it will be a better life. If you can imagine a life without the pain and sorrow, the death and the grief that haunt us here and now, a life in God's presence, you have the picture of the new life that God promises.

Eternal Life Starting Now

Within Judaism modern thinkers and writers have suggested other ways in which we gain immortality even now. One suggestion is *biological immortality.* We live on through the recycling of the chemicals in our bodies into the soil or through the great drama of the human race or through children. Jewish families tend to name a son or daughter after a grandparent so that the grandparent's name is repeated over and over, from generation to generation. Further, Jewish people identify themselves with generations past, sharing in the joys of those God brought out of the land of Egypt and in the sufferings of those who experienced the Holocaust. A second method is *immortality through influence.* Parents, teachers, writers, friends continue to exist in the ways they have affected positively the lives of others. As the role models are remembered, they live on. The third method is *immortality through deeds.* Jewish tradition speaks of the "merit of the fathers," a recognition that the goodness of previous generations contributes to the well-being of people in the present and in the future. By the same token, the present generation is called to contribute good deeds on behalf of those in the past who cherished high ideals. In so doing, the entire community lives according to the promise of God.

Christians also speak of eternal life beginning here and now, but in a different sense.

> *God's will is for life, God promises life, and God will grant new life beyond the grave.*

Based on the Gospel according to John, they believe that once a person is baptized, eternal life has already begun. It is a new birth, a new life. Death is a temporary interruption, of course, but life will resume at the time of resurrection. This understanding brings comfort to those who are facing death, for they can feel confident they have already begun to live eternally and will continue to do so after death.

These views regarding life after death arise not simply because people wish so strongly for existence to continue. They emerge because Jews and Christians believe God's will is for life, God promises life, and God will grant new life beyond the grave.

That hope is basic to Judaism and Christianity. It is also the hope that is offered to you freely by a loving, forgiving, and gracious God.

Chapter Six

REINVESTING

EVENTUALLY the moment comes when you are ready to put the pieces together and move on. You will accept the finality of the death you are grieving and prepare yourself for new directions. That intentional movement from grief toward a productive life is called reinvesting.

The Challenges of the Journey

The duration of the period of mourning varies from person to person. A broken limb mends in a certain number of weeks, but a broken heart might last for years. During your mourning you might experience times when you function well, able to accept your loss and move onward. At other times your emotions will run rampant, and depression and despondency might prevent you from journeying forward.

You will take the first steps toward a new beginning with understandable caution. You might be walking on new ground or into territory you have not entered for years. You might be afraid of failing or being rejected or getting hurt. You might also wonder if it is the right time. Has sufficient time elapsed for your mourning to change to constructive movement? Will you dishonor the memory of your beloved by setting out on a new course? What will others think? Can you have a good time without feeling guilty? Establish new relationships? Pursue happiness? Will you appear uncaring and insensitive to friends and members of your family?

Reinvesting might require you to develop new skills or to use your old skills and your time in different ways. Your schedule has changed since your loved one died. You can no longer share that time together you enjoyed so much. What do you do with your time now? Somehow you need to fill in the gaps. You need to spend time with other people, give yourself the freedom to enjoy their company, and venture into new interests. While you might experience some guilt and ambivalence about enjoying yourself with other people, you should comfort yourself with the realization

---

Taking the first steps along the journey toward reinvesting requires courage, hope, and faith.

---

that remaining alone will lead to increased emptiness and loneliness.

Taking the first steps along the journey toward reinvesting requires courage, hope, and faith. Activities you and your beloved shared, places you went together, conversations you held — all these have a special place in your heart. You might be uncomfortable doing those special things with someone else. You will need to decide whether revisiting old memories is helpful or hurtful, but you might consider that you can honor your beloved by repeating what you had enjoyed together.

When you go out with other people, especially with couples, you might feel like the fifth wheel on the wagon, because they were the people you previously related to as a couple. You might feel they are now inviting you only to be kind. But you yourself are a person of value and dignity. You yourself have as much to give to others as they have to give you. You have traits and gifts that enable you to contribute to conversations and activities and causes.

As a widow or widower you might eventually reach the point where you are willing to socialize with members of the opposite sex. It is not unhealthy to establish such relationships.

> *Your beloved would only want the best for you.*

Making a new life with one of them — if that be your desire — does not dishonor your loved one. It might even be a sign that you enjoyed your beloved so much that you need another partner to find the same kind of fulfillment, to reestablish your sense of wholeness, to love and be loved again. God did not make us to be alone but to live together in community, as partners within the larger society.

No matter what might have been said in the midst of suffering and in the face of dying, your beloved would only want the best for you. If he loved you, he wants you to be happy. If she loved you, she wants what is good for the rest of your life. You have the freedom and the challenge of making a new life for yourself, and in the beauty and dignity and value of your life, your beloved is honored in death just as in life.

Such a venture into a committed relationship might be out of the question at the moment.

God can make good out of the worst of situations.

You might need to crawl before you can walk and to walk before you can leap. You might take two steps backward for every one forward for a while. What is important is that the overall direction be forward. Movement builds if you persevere toward healing and reinvesting. In the meantime be patient with yourself and with others. The journey itself will help you build confidence and reinforce for you the possibility of new directions.

The Unfathomable Work of God

Never underestimate the power of God.

God can make good out of the worst of situations. Through the darkest of clouds God can break through with light and joy, transforming disaster into new opportunities.

God can use the tragedy of death to teach you about life: how to value it, how to make the most of the time allotted to us mortals, how to seize the moment rather than postpone participation until the opportunity for joy is lost.

God can work through the death of your beloved to enable you to be more decisive and confident. You might come to realize you have strengths and abilities you never knew you had and to make contributions to the lives of others you never imagined.

Out of the sorrow of death God reinforces existing relationships and creates new ones. In the process you discover people who care about you and others to whom you can reach out. You find that life can be a joy once again because God has not allowed you to remain isolated and alone.

Out of death God can make a meaningful life for you here and now, just as God will make life out of death at the time of the resurrection. The hope in God's eternal promise enables you and others to live even now to the glory and praise of God.

Living Life Under God

We have seen throughout this book that part of the process of grieving when a loved one has died involves struggling with the question *why*, directing anger at everyone connected with death, and wrestling with the haunting issues of guilt and loneliness. It is no wonder that people despair in the face of death.

Taking your grief to God, however, allows you to live a life filled with promise.

Certainly many of the mysteries remain. You will continue to live with some unanswered

---

> *God gives you the strength to continue in this life as a person of dignity and challenges you to reinvest your talents, your gifts, even yourself.*

---

questions. You will never know *why* the death of your beloved occurred at this time in your life together. You will never be satisfied with the unknowns about life after death. You will never feel certain that you have all the pieces together.

In the midst of the unknowns, however, God gives you what you need to move onward. God assures you of being present with you, even when you feel most alone. God comforts you when you are angry, even angry at God, for the upheaval this death has caused in your life. God forgives you for whatever you feel you did or did not do. God promises you new life, not as a substitute for death but through it, a life that will be blessed and joyous. In the meantime God gives you the strength to continue in this life as a person of dignity and challenges you to reinvest your talents, your gifts, even yourself.

The more you acknowledge that God has been that source of strength for you, the more beneficial your suffering will have been. To admit to yourself that God's power pulled you through your weakness will enable you to continue through life with the conviction that God will be there in the future also. To tell others about the strength of God during your difficult times will provide them with support and direction when they feel the way you did.

In your grief God has given you wondrous gifts. In your journey onward God also gives you challenging opportunities. The love and presence and promises of God can help you make enough sense out of your sorrow to live a life that is fulfilling and productive. That kind of life honors your beloved. Above all, it honors and praises God.